D1427914

# Try Not To

# Laugh

# Challenge

## Summer Campfire Edition

## Joke Book

# Copyright 2019 by Hayden Fox - All rights reserved.

This document is geared towards providing exact and reliable information in regards to the topic and issue covered. The publication is sold with the idea that the publisher is not required to render an accounting, officially permitted, or otherwise, qualified services. If advice is necessary, legal or professional, a practiced individual in the profession should be ordered.

- From a Declaration of Principles which was accepted and approved equally by a Committee of the American Bar Association and a Committee of Publishers and Associations.

In no way is it legal to reproduce, duplicate, or transmit any part of this document by either electronic means or in printed format. Recording of this publication is strictly prohibited and any storage of this document is not allowed unless with written permission from the publisher. All rights reserved.

The information provided herein is stated to be truthful and consistent, in that any liability, in terms of inattention or otherwise, by any usage or abuse of any policies, processes, or directions contained within is the solitary and utter responsibility of the recipient reader. Under no circumstances will any legal responsibility or blame be held against the publisher for any reparation, damages, or monetary loss due to the information herein, either directly or indirectly.

Respective authors and companies own all copyrights not held by the publisher.

The information herein is offered for informational purposes solely and is universal as so. The presentation of the information is without a contract or any type of guarantee assurance.

The trademarks that are used are without any consent, and the publication of the trademark is without permission or backing by the trademark owner. All trademarks and brands within this book are for clarifying purposes only and are owned by the owners themselves, not affiliated with this document.

# How To Play

### Step 1

Split into two teams whether that be boys vs girls, kids vs parents, or any mix of your choice. If possible, also assign one person as a referee. You can also do 1 vs 1!

### Step 2

Decide who gets to go first. Which team can do the most pushups? Which team can guess the number between 1 and 10 from someone not playing the game? Or just a good old fashioned rock paper scissors?

## *Step 3*

The starting team has to tell a joke from the book. You can say the joke however you like and animate it too with funny faces, gestures, or whatever else.

## *Step 4*

If everyone on the opposing team laughs, the other team gets a point! Set a limit for how many points it takes to win and the first team to reach the limit, wins!

# What do you call a dear with no eyes?

*(In a southern accent) I have no idear!*

# How does a pirate prefer to travel?

*By ARRRRRR-V*

# What do you say to a one legged hitch hiker?

*Hop in!*

# Why did the duck say bang?

*Because he was a firequacker!*

# Why don't lobsters share?

*They're shellfish.*

# What is brown and sticky?

*A stick!*

# What do you get when you cross a dinosaur with fireworks?

*Dinomite*

# What's tree plus tree?

*Sticks*

# What do you call a guy with no arms and legs on the side of a mountain?

*Cliff*

# What do you call a woman with no arms and legs on the beach?

*Sandy*

# What did the mushroom say when he wasn't invited to the party?

*But I'm such a fun-gi!*

# My brother and I were fighting each other yesterday...

*It was in tents!*

# I asked Google how to start a campfire without tools...

*It gave me 20 million matches!*

# I love campfire smoke so much...

*It brings tears to my eyes.*

# Want to hear my campfire jokes?

*They're straight fire!*

# I got a job as a human cannonball...

*I was immediately fired.*

# What's the difference between a duck and George Washington?

*One has a bill on his face while the other has his face on a bill!*

# Why didn't the Mexican archer fire his bow?

*He didn't habanero!*

# I never go camping with only one other person...

*It's just two in tents!*

# What do camping and fancy hotels have in common?

*Toilet trees are complementary!*

# What do you get when you cross Captain America with the Incredible Hulk?

*The Star Spangled Banner*

# What sound does a nut make when it sneezes?

*Cashew!*

# I went to buy some camouflage trousers...

*But I couldn't find any!*

# I've just come back from a once in a lifetime trip...

*Never again!*

# What did the two fish in the tank say to each other?

*How do you drive this thing??*

# What's orange and sounds like a parrot?

*A carrot*

# I slept like a log last night...

*I woke up in the campfire.*

# What was General Washington's favorite tree?

*Infantry*

# What do you call cheese that isn't yours?

*Nacho cheese*

# Why did the toilet paper roll down the hill?

*To get to the bottom!*

# What do bears call campers in sleeping bags?

*Soft tacos*

# Why did Humpty Dumpty like camping in autumn?

*Because he had a great fall!*

# Did you hear about the camper who broke his left arm and leg?

*He's all right now.*

# What do you call a camper without a nose or body?

*Nobody knows!*

# What do you get when you cross a fish and two elephants?

*Swimming trunks*

# What do clouds do when they get rich?

*They make it rain*

# How do trees access the internet?

*They log in.*

# What do you call a bear with no teeth?

*A gummy bear*

# How do you catch a squirrel?

*Climb a tree and act nutty!*

# Why is a river rich?

*Because it has two banks.*

# How do trees have so many friends?

*They branch out.*

# What did the beaver say to the log?

*It's been nice gnawing you!*

# What is a tree's favorite drink?

*Root Beer*

# What was the American colonists' favorite tea?

*Liberty*

# What was the most popular dance in early American history?

*Indepen-dance*

# What do you call a fake noodle?

*An impasta*

# What do you call a sketchy Italian neighbourhood?

*The spaghetto*

# Why don't skeletons go trick or treating?

*They have no body to go with!*

# I used to hate facial hair...

*But then it grew on me.*

# Did you get a hair cut?

*No I got them all cut!*

# What does a nosey pepper do?

*It gets jalapeño business!*

# Why shouldn't you tell an egg a joke?

*Because it might crack up!*

# What's a hen's favorite veggie?

*Eggplant*

# What's a scarecrow's favorite fruit?

*Strawberry*

# What sounds does a metal frog make?

## *Rivet Rivet*

# What kind of vitamins do fish like?

*Vitamin Sea*

# Why didn't the teddy bear want dessert?

*Because it was stuffed!*

# How do you put an astronaut baby to sleep?

*Rocket*

# What did the baseball mitt say to the baseball?

*Catch ya later!*

# Why do witches fly on broomsticks?

*Vacuum cleaners are too heavy.*

# Why do you tell actors to break a leg?

*Because every movie needs a cast.*

# Why did the student eat his homework?

*His teacher told him it was a piece of cake!*

# What do you get when mix history and oil?

*Ancient grease*

# What does Thor receive every month?

*A high electricity bill*

# What is a sheep's favorite sports car?

*A lamb-borghini*

# What becomes infinitely bigger when you rotate it 90 degrees?

*The number eight*

# How many feet are in a yard?

*It depends on how many people are standing in it!*

# Why didn't the barber cross the road?

*He didn't believe in shortcuts.*

# What do you call a smart dinosaur?

*A thesaurus*

# Where do TV's go to vacation?

*Remote islands*

# Why was the math book always worried?

*Because it had so many problems!*

# Did you hear about the joke of Liberty Bell?

*Yeah, it cracked me up!*

# What colonists told the most jokes?

*Punsylvanians*

# What did one flag say to the other flag?

*Nothing, it just waved!*

# A man asked me to help him check his balance at the bank today...

*So I pushed him over!*

## What do you call security guards at the Samsung store?

*Guardians of the Galaxy*

# What's a ten letter word that starts with gas?

*Automobile*

# Where do sharks go camping?

*Finland*

# Why don't mummies go camping?

*They're afraid to sit back and unwind!*

# Have you heard the joke about the skunk and the camping trip?

*Never mind, it really stinks!*

# Where did the sheep family go for vacation?

*The Baaaahamas*

# Where do birds like to go on vacation?

*The Canary Islands*

# What did the lake say to the campers?

*Nothing, it just waved.*

# What does Barry Allen always take on his camping trips?

*His FLASHlight*

# How do campers access the internet?

*They log in.*

# Why was the fish blushing?

*It saw the lake's bottom.*

# What type of witches like to camp on the beach?

*Sandwitches*

# Why didn't the bike go camping?

*It was two tired!*

Enjoying the book so far? Let us know what you think by leaving a review!

What has been your favorite joke from the book thus far?

# What did one flower say to the other?

*What's up Bud?*

# Where did the seaweed look for a job?

*The Kelp Wanted section*

# What do you call a wolf that uses bad language?

*A swearwolf*

# What did Venus say to Saturn?

*Give me a ring sometime!*

# Why did the cow cross the road?

*To get to the udder side!*

# What do you call a cow that munches on your grass?

*A lawn moo-er*

# When is the moon the heaviest?

*When it's full!*

# Why did the leaf go to the doctor?

*It was feeling green.*

# What kind of shorts do clouds wear?

*Thunderwear*

# What kind of tree can you grow in your hand?

*A palm tree*

# What did the little tree say to the big tree?

*Leaf me alone!*

# Why does the sun have to go to school?

*To get brighter.*

# What do you call a dinosaur that's sleeping?

*A dino-snore*

# What do you get when you cross a vampire and a snowman?

*Frostbite*

# What did one plate say to the other plate?

*Dinner is on me!*

# Why did the cookie go to the hospital?

*Because he felt crummy!*

# What time did you have to go to the dentist?

*At tooth-hurty.*

# Why did the king go to the dentist?

*To get a new crown.*

# How is a judge like a teacher?

*They both hand out long sentences.*

# Why did the clock go to the principal's office?

*For tocking too much.*

# What kind of roads do ghosts look for?

*Dead ends*

# What do snowmen like to eat for breakfast?

*Frosted Flakes*

# Where does Superman love to shop?

*At the supermarket!*

# What do you give a sick lemon?

*Lemon-aid*

# What do you call a cow with no legs?

*Ground beef*

# What did the burger name his daughter?

*Patty*

# What is the most musical part of a fish?

*The scales*

# What genre of music do balloons hate?

*Pop*

# What is a skeleton's favorite instrument?

*The trom-bone*

# Why was the musician arrested?

*Because she got in some treble!*

# What rock group has 4 guys who can't sing?

*Mount Rushmore*

# What do lawyers wear to court?

*Lawsuits*

# What lights up a football stadium?

*A football match*

# Why was the baby strawberry sad?

*Because her parents were in a jam!*

# Why shouldn't you write with a broken pencil?

*Because it's pointless.*

# What do you call a sleeping bull?

*A bulldozer!*

# What do you call a belt with a watch on it?

*A waist of time*

# What do you call bears with no ears?

*B*

# Where do pencils go for vacation?

*Pencil-vania*

# What did the judge say when the skunk walked into court?

*Odor in the court!*

# What is the best day to go to the beach?

*Sunday*

# What bow can't be tied?

*A rainbow*

# Where did the computer go to dance?

*To the disc-o!*

# Do fish go on vacation?

*No, because they're always in school!*

# Why do fish like to eat worms?

*Because they're hooked on them!*

# What is a shark's favorite sandwich?

*Peanut Butter and Jellyfish*

# What is a frog's favorite frozen treat?

*Hopsicles*

# What is a killer whale's favorite type of music?

*An orca-stra*

# Why did the robot go on vacation?

*To recharge his batteries.*

# What did the grape say when he was stepped on?

*Nothing. He just gave a little wine.*

# What did one strawberry say to the other?

*How did we get in this jam?*

# What do you say to a sweaty puppy?

*You're one hot dog!*

# What do sheep do on sunny days?

*Baaaaa-becue*

# Where does a ship go when it's sick?

*To the dock*

# Why do fish swim in salt water?

*Because pepper makes them sneeze!*

# What did the beach say when the tide came in?

*Long time no sea!*

# What's that new pirate movie rated?

*ARRRRR!*

# What's black and white and red all over?

*A zebra with a sunburn*

# What do you call a snowman in July?

*A puddle*

# Why didn't the elephant bring a suitcase?

*Because he already has a trunk.*

# What do frogs like to drink on a hot summer day?

*Croak-o-cola*

# Why do fish never make good tennis players?

*Because they never get close to the net!*

# When do you go at red and stop at green?

*When eating a watermelon!*

# What did the pig say at the beach on a hot summer day?

*I'm bacon!*

# What does the sun drink out of?

*Sun glasses*

# Which letter is the coolest?

*Iced T*

# Why did the dolphin cross the beach?

*To get to the other tide.*

# What was the first animal in space?

*The cow that jumped over the moon*

# How can you tell a vampire has a cold?

*They start coffin!*

# How are false teeth like stars?

*They come out at night.*

# How do scientists freshen their breath?

*With experi-mints*

# How does a cucumber become a pickle?

*By going through a jarring experience.*

# What time is it when the clock strikes 13?

*Time to get a new clock.*

# How do you make a tissue dance?

*You put a little boogie in it!*

# Why did the dinosaur cross the road?

*Because the chicken hadn't been born yet.*

# Why can't Elsa have a balloon?

*Because she will let it go!*

# What building in New York has the most stories?

*The Public Library*

# How does the moon cut his hair?

*Eclipse it!*

# What is a tornado's favorite game to play?

*Twister*

# What animal is always at a baseball game?

*A bat*

# What do you call two giraffes colliding?

*A girrafic jam*

# How do you pay for parking in space?

*A parking meteor*

# Would February March?

*No but April May.*

# What day of the week are most twins born on?

*Twosday*

# Why isn't there a clock in the library?

*Because it tocks too much.*

# What kind of vegetables are angry?

*Steamed vegetables*

# Why didn't the koala bear get the job?

*She was over-koala-fied!*

# What did the traffic light say to the truck?

*Don't look, I'm changing!*

# What did the flower say after it told a joke?

*I was just pollen your leg.*

# What time do ducks wake up?

*At the quack of dawn.*

# Why did the giraffes get bad grades?

*She had her head in the clouds.*

# Why did the superhero flush the toilet?

*Because it was his doody.*

# Why was the broom running late?

*It overswept.*

# What does bread do on vacation?

*Loaf around*

# Why was 6 so mad at 7?

*Because 7 ate 9.*

# What happens when you cross a pie with a snake?

*A pie-thon*

# What haircut do bees like?

*A buzzzzzcut*

# What do evil hens lay?

*Deviled eggs!*

# Why are robots never afraid?

*They have nerves of steel.*

# Why did the tomato blush?

*It saw the salad dressing!*

# What do you call a fish without an eye?

*A fsh*

# How do you throw a party in space?

*You planet.*

# How do pickles enjoy a day out?

*They relish it.*

# Why didn't the orange win the race?

*It ran out of juice!*

Thank you for reading! If you enjoyed the book, leave us a review and let us know what you liked or what you would like to see next.

As a special bonus, enjoy this exclusive preview of one our other popular titles!

**250**

**Would You**

**Rather**

**Questions**

*A Clean, Fun, and Hilarious Activity Book for Kids, Teens, and Adults*

# 250 Would You Rather Questions

## Questions

A Clean, Fun, and Hilarious

Activity Book For Kids, Teens,

and Adults

# How To Play

### Step 1

Split into two teams whether that be boys vs girls, kids vs parents, or any mix of your choice. If possible, also assign one person as a referee.

### Step 2

Decide who gets to go first. Which team can do the most pushups? Which team can guess the number between 1 and 10 from someone not playing the game? Or just a good old fashioned rock paper scissors?

## Step 3

The starting team has to ask a question from the book and the opposing team has 10 seconds to not only choose an option but to also give a meaningful reason as to why they chose what they did. The referee decides whether the answer is acceptable.

## Step 4

The team can discuss their answer together but only one player can give the answer. The person answering has to alternate every turn.

## Step 5

If the player who is answering can't choose or give a good reason then that player is out for the game and can't answer anymore or be involved in the team discussion.

## Step 6

Repeat until all players are eliminated.

# Questions

1. Would you rather live one life that lasts 1000 years or 10 lives that last 100 years each?

2. Would you rather use eye drops made of vinegar or toilet paper made of sandpaper?

3. Would you rather be 4'0 or 8'0?

4. Would you rather be super strong or super fast?

5. Would you rather take a guaranteed $120,000 or take a 50/50 chance at $1,000,000?

6. Would you rather be in constant pain or have a constant itch?

7. Would you rather go forward or backward in time?

8. Would you rather never be able to take a hot shower again or eat hot food again?

9. Would you rather never play or play but always lose?

10. Would you rather be a vegetarian or only be able to eat meat?

11. Would you rather be a
    chronic farter or chronic
    burper?

12. Would you rather be
    deaf or mute?

13. Would you rather have a third eye or third arm?

14. Would you rather age from the neck up only or neck down only?

15. Would you rather be only able to shout or whisper?

16. Would you rather never touch an electronic device again or a human?

17. Would you rather have a mediocre short term memory or bad long term memory?

18. Would you rather have 2 wishes today or 3 wishes in 5 years?

19. Would you rather drink a glass of expired milk or pee your pants in public?

20. Would you rather hang out with a few friends or go to a big party?

21. Would you rather master every language or every instrument?

22. Would you rather have to wear formal clothes for the rest of your life or informal?

23. Would you rather eat a stick of butter or a teaspoon of cinnamon?

24. Would you rather have the ability to read people's minds or fly?

25. Would you rather have your house always have its lights on or off?

26. Would you rather be ignorant and happy or knowledgeable but not content?

27. Would you rather have to take cold showers to be clean or never be clean at all?

28. Would you rather lick someone's armpit or lick your floor?

29. Would you rather have your flight be delayed by 18 hours or lose your luggage?

30. Would you rather be an amazing player on the losing team or the worst player on the winning team?

31. Would you rather be ugly and marry a good looking person or be good looking and marry an ugly person?

32. Would you rather be a genius in a world of morons or a moron in a world of geniuses?

33. Would you rather be stuck in a house alone or with someone you hate?

34. Would you rather dump someone or have them dump you?

35. Would you rather be a parent or child?

36. Would you rather lose your arms or legs?

37. Would you rather be homeless for a year or go to jail for a year?

38. Would you rather go without the internet for a month or transportation?

39. Would you rather be homeless or be without family and friends?

40. Would you rather be really hairy or completely bald?

41. Would you rather eat healthy or exercise every day?

42. Would you rather lose half your hearing or half your hair?

43. Would you rather look weak and actually be strong or look strong and actually be weak?

44. Would you rather be miserable but rich at a job or love what you do but be poor?

45. Would you rather be rich and ugly or poor and good looking?

46. Would you rather be in constant pain or have a constant itch?

47. Would you rather be unable to ask questions or unable to give any answers?

48. Would you rather save the life of someone close to you or 7 random strangers?

49. Would you rather have a dragon or be a dragon?

50. Would you rather be literate or be able to read minds and be illiterate?

If you enjoyed the book, be sure to check out our other books by searching "Hayden Fox" on Amazon!

29922537R00077

Printed in Great
Britain
by Amazon